VIRTUE STORIES

Never give Up

Lalita Iyer

Om KIDZ
An imprint of Om Books International

Ishaan watched his three-year-old sister carefully. There! She's done it again, he thought.

He pressed his thumbs against his middle fingers, took a moment, and then brushed them against each other. No click.

He tried again. And again.

But his fingers refused to click in that nice 'click-click-click' manner that he was so keen to master.

His sister Ina was lolling on the bean bag and watching TV, but he knew she was watching him really, so he ignored her.

'Like this,' she said and clicked her fingers loudly.

He turned his back to her. Ina was so annoying.

Sometimes, she would start winking with both eyes alternately - he never knew how she did it! That was even more annoying.

Such a show off, he thought. But I am going to keep trying till I get it...

He held his hands in his lap and practised the clicks. His fingers softly and silently brushed past each other. He decided to give it a break and pressed his hands together, giving them a gentle massage.

'Like this,' Ina called out. This time he looked over. She held up her hands, pressed her thumb against her middle fingers and released! Click!

Ishaan held up his right hand. He pressed his thumb against his middle finger. He took a deep breath.

The fingers passed by each other in total silence. Ina winked at him, first with her left eye, then with her right. ‘Don’t give up,’ she chuckled, and turned back to watch TV. Ishaan did the only thing he could do. He stuck his tongue out at her!

Bored, he picked up the two ping-pong balls on the table and randomly started throwing them in the air. He soon realised he could throw both up and pick them up at the same time. Let me try something else, he thought. Ina was now watching him very closely.

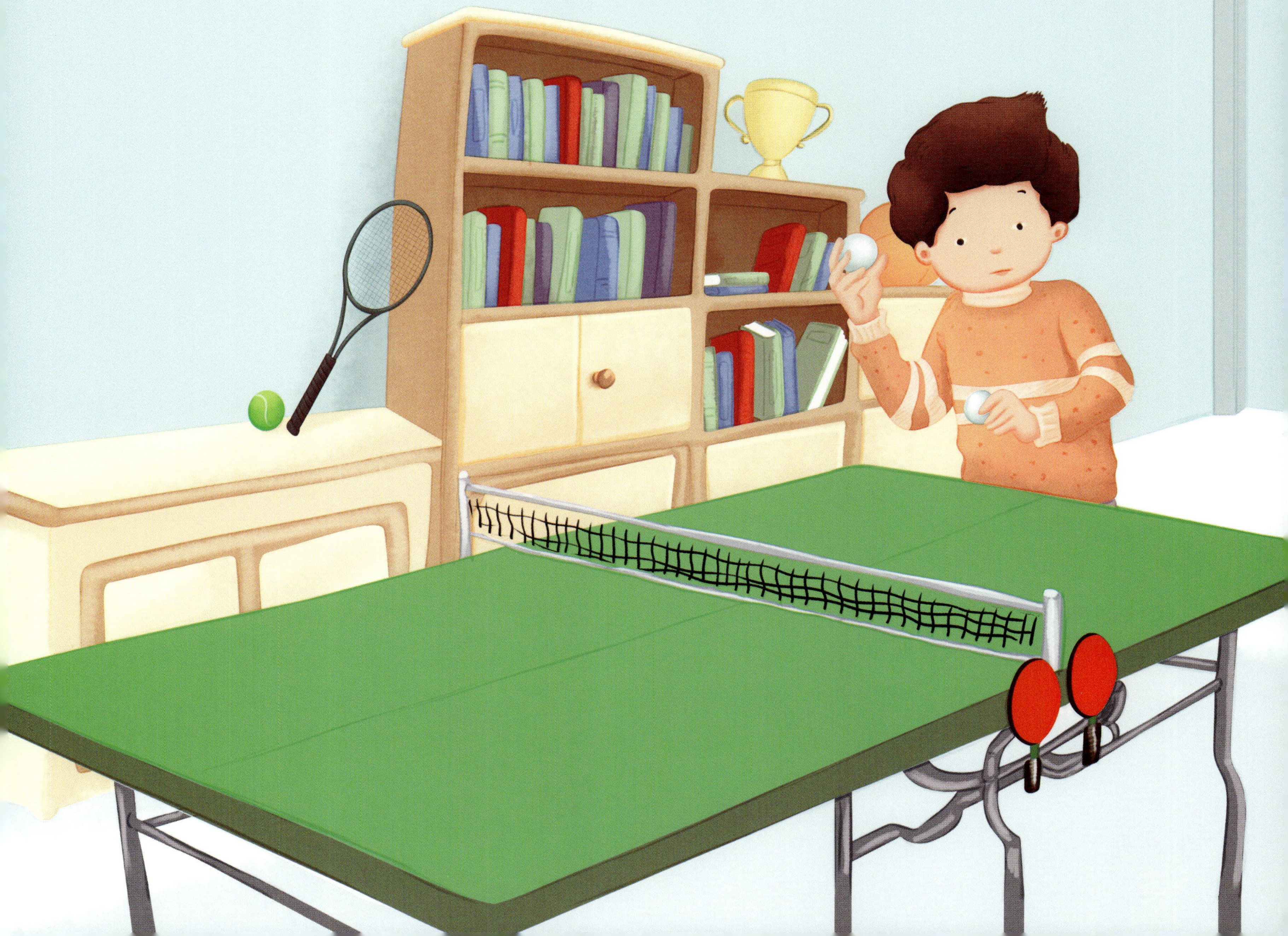

Ishaan now tried again, hoping it wouldn't slip. It didn't. Balls up in the air, Ishaan's eyes were shifting from one ball to the next, as one went up and the other went down. And he kept on, and on, and on at it.

Next he threw one ball a second after the other, and soon caught them in the opposite hand. Ina clapped when it happened. 'Hey, that's called juggling! I want to learn too!'

Ina was clapping loudly, cheering her big brother on, who was now officially, her favourite juggler!